SCOTLAND'S NEW WRITING THEATRE

Traverse Theatre Company

Night Time

by Selma Dimitrijević

cast in order of appearance

Chris	Kananu Kirimi
Frank	John Kazek
Thomas	David Ireland
Bowman	Benny Young

Director	Lorne Campbell
Designer	Jon Bausor
Lighting Designer	Jon Clark
Composer	Philip Pinsky
Voice Coach	Ros Steen
Stage Manager	Lee Davis
Deputy Stage Manager	Christabel Anderson
Assistant Stage Manager	Rob Armstrong
Wardrobe Supervisor	Victoria Young

**first performed at the Traverse Theatre,
Friday 20 July 2007**

a Traverse Theatre Commission

THE TRAVERSE

Artistic Director Philip Howard

A Rolls-Royce machine for promoting new Scottish drama across Europe and beyond.
(The Scotsman)

The Traverse's commissioning process embraces a spirit of innovation and risk-taking that has launched the careers of many of Scotland's best-known writers including John Byrne, David Greig, David Harrower and Liz Lochhead. It is unique in Scotland in that it fulfils the crucial role of providing the infrastructure, professional support and expertise to ensure the development of a dynamic theatre culture for Scotland.

The importance of the Traverse is difficult to overestimate . . . without the theatre, it is difficult to imagine Scottish playwriting at all. (Sunday Times)

From its conception in the 1960s, the Traverse has remained a pivotal venue during the Edinburgh Festival. It receives enormous critical and audience acclaim for its programming, as well as regularly winning awards. From 2001–05, Traverse Theatre productions of *Gagarin Way* by Gregory Burke, *Outlying Islands* by David Greig, *Iron* by Rona Munro, *The People Next Door* by Henry Adam, *Shimmer* by Linda McLean, *When the Bulbul Stopped Singing* by Raja Shehadeh and *East Coast Chicken Supper* by Martin J Taylor have won Fringe First or Herald Angel Awards (and occasionally both).

2006 was a record-breaking year for the Traverse as their Festival programme *Passion* picked up an incredible 14 awards including a Herald Angel Award for their own production of *Strawberries in January* by Evelyne de la Chenelière in a version by Rona Munro.

The Traverse Theatre has established itself as Scotland's leading exponent of new writing, with a reputation that extends worldwide. (The Scotsman)

The Traverse's success isn't limited to the Edinburgh stage, since 2001 Traverse productions of *Gagarin Way, Outlying Islands, Iron, The People Next Door, When the Bulbul Stopped Singing, The Slab Boys Trilogy, Mr Placebo* and *Helmet* have toured not only within Scotland and the UK, but in Sweden, Norway, the Balkans, Germany, USA, Iran, Jordan and Canada. Immediately following the 2006 festival, the Traverse's production of *Petrol Jesus Nightmare #5 (In the Time of the Messiah)* by Henry Adam was invited to perform at the International Festival in Priština, Kosovo and won the Jury Special Award for Production.

One of Europe's most important homes for new plays.
(Sunday Herald)

Now in its 14th year, the Traverse's annual Highlands & Islands tour is a crucial strand of their work. This commitment to Scottish touring has taken plays from their Edinburgh home to audiences all over Scotland. The Traverse has criss-crossed the nation performing at diverse locations from Shetland to Dumfries, Aberdeen to Benbecula. The Traverse's 2005 production *I was a Beautiful Day* was commissioned to open the new An Lanntair Arts Centre in Stornoway, Isle of Lewis.

Auld Reekie's most important theatre. (The Times)

The Traverse's work with young people is of supreme importance and takes the form of encouraging playwriting through its flagship education project *Class Act*, as well as the Young Writers' Group. *Class Act* is now in its 17th year and gives pupils the opportunity to develop their plays with professional playwrights and work with directors and actors to see the finished piece performed on stage at the Traverse. This year, for the fourth year running, the project also took place in Russia. In 2004 *Articulate*, a large scale project based on the *Class Act* model, took place in West Dunbartonshire working with 11 to 14-year-olds. The hugely successful Young Writers' Group is open to new writers aged between 18 and 25 and the fortnightly meetings are led by a professional playwright.

The Traverse has an unrivalled reputation for producing contemporary theatre of the highest quality, invention and energy, and for its dedication to new writing. (Scotland on Sunday)

The Traverse is committed to working with international playwrights and, in 2005, produced *In the Bag* by Wang Xiaoli in a version by Ronan O'Donnell, the first-ever full production of a contemporary Chinese play in the UK. This project was part of the successful Playwrights in Partnership scheme, which unites international and Scottish writers, and brings the most dynamic new global voices to the Edinburgh stage. Other international Traverse partnerships have included work in Québec, Norway, Finland, France, Italy, Portugal and Japan.

www.traverse.co.uk

To find out about ways in which you can support the work of the Traverse please contact our Development Department
0131 228 3223 or development@traverse.co.uk

Charity No. SC002368

COMPANY BIOGRAPHIES

Jon Bausor (Designer)

Jon trained at Exeter College of Art and Motley Theatre Design Course. For the Traverse: *Melody, In the Bag*. Other designs for theatre include *Julius Caesar, Terminus* (Abbey Theatre, Dublin); *Scenes From The Back Of Beyond* (Royal Court); *The Soldier's Tale* (The Old Vic); *Notes From Underground* (West End); *James and the Giant Peach* (Octagon Theatre, Bolton); *The Great Highway* (Gate Theatre, London); *The Hoxton Story* (Red Room Productions); *Cymbeline, Macbeth* (Regent's Park Open Air Theatre); *The Last Waltz Season* (Oxford Stage Company/Arcola Theatre); *Frankenstein* (Derby Playhouse); *Baghdad Wedding, Shrieks of Laughter* (Soho Theatre); *Bread and Butter* (Tricycle Theatre); *Sanctuary, The Tempest* (Royal National Theatre); *Winners, Interior, The Exception and The Rule, The New Tenant, The Soul of Chien-Nu Leaves Her Body* (Young Vic); *The Taming of the Shrew* (Theatre Royal Plymouth/Thelma Holt Ltd national tour); *Carver* (Arcola/RADA). Designs for dance include *Snow White in Black* (Phoenix Dance Theatre – Dance Critics Circle Award); *Echo and Narcissus, Ghosts, Before The Tempest, Sophie, Stateless* and *Asyla* (Linbury Theatre, Royal Opera House); *Mixtures* (English National Ballet); *Non Exeunt* (George Piper Dances/Sadler's Wells), *Marjorie's World Unhinged* (Tilted); *Firebird* (Bern Ballet, Switzerland); Designs for opera include *The Queen of Spades* (Edinburgh Festival Theatre); *Cosi Fan Tutti* (Handmade Opera) and *King Arthur* (New Chamber Opera).

Lorne Campbell (Director)

Lorne trained at the Traverse Theatre on the Channel 4 Theatre Director's Scheme from 2002-2004 and has been Associate Director since 2005. Other training: RSAMD (Mdra) and Liverpool John Moores (BAHons). Directing credits for the Traverse include the world premieres of *Carthage Must Be Destroyed* and *The Nest* by Alan Wilkins, *Distracted* by Morna Pearson, *White Point* by David Priestly, *Broke* by David Lescot in a version by Iain F MacLeod, *Melody* by Douglas Maxwell and *In the Bag* by Xiaoli Wang in a version by Ronan O'Donnell. Lorne was also Associate Director for *East Coast Chicken Supper* by Martin J Taylor and *The People Next Door* by Henry Adam (Balkan Tour 2004). Other theatre credits include: *Brokenville* (British Council/Young Audience's Ensemble of Togliatti) *The Dumb Waiter, Death and the Maiden, An Evening with Damon Runyon, A Comedy of Errors, As You Like It, Journey's End* (Forge Theatre); *The Chairs* (RSAMD); *The Cheviot, The Stag and the Black, Black Oil* (Taigh Chearsabhagh).

Jon Clark (Lighting Designer)

Jon studied Theatre Design at Bretton Hall, Leeds University (BAHons). Recent theatre credits include *How Much is Your Iron?*, *The Jewish Wife* (Young Vic); *Pinter's People* (Mick Perrin Productions/Theatre Royal, Haymarket); *Food* (The Imaginary Body); *The Soldier's Tale* (Motion Group/The Old Vic); *Gone To Earth* (Shared Experience/The Old Vic); *Underworld* (Frantic Assembly); *Tale That Wags The Dog* (AandBC/Drum Theatre, Plymouth); *Mandragora* (Tara Arts/Tron Theatre); *A Collier's Friday Night* (Oxford Drama School/BAC). Design for Opera includes *The Barber of Seville, L' Elisir D'Amore, Cosi Fan Tutte* (Grange Park Opera). Revival Lighting Design for Opera includes *Jenufa* (ENO/Washington National Opera). Recent design for dance includes *Sorry For The Missiles* (Scottish Dance Theatre); *Into The Hoods, BoxBeat* (ZooNation Dance); *REAL* (ACE Dance); *Mountains are Mountains* (Phillipp Gehmacher, Vienna); *Embryonic Dreams* (Pyromania). Associate Lighting Design includes *Evita* (Adelphi Theatre, London).

Selma Dimitrijević (Writer)

Selma is a Croatian-born writer, translator and dramaturg now based in Edinburgh. Her most recent theatre work includes *Game Theory* for Ek Performance, co-written with Pamela Carter (Traverse, Festival 2007); *Re:Union* for 7:84 Theatre Company (Scottish Tour, Spring 2007) and *Broken* for *Play, Pie & Pint* Season (Oran Mor, 2006). As a translator, Selma has worked on plays and novels by David Harrower, Enda Walsh, Irvine Welsh, James Kelman and Salman Rushdie. Last November, she took part in *Cubed³*, the Traverse Theatre's emerging artists season, on the Writers Residency Programme.

David Ireland (*Thomas*)

David trained at RSAMD. For the Traverse: the *Tilt* triple bill. Other theatre includes *The Talented Mr Ripley, Cinderella, If Destroyed True, The Visit, Merlin the Magnificent, A Lie of the Mind* (Dundee Rep); *My Old Man* (Magnetic North); *Revenge* (Tinderbox); *The Lieutenant of Inishmore* (RSC); *Lament* (Suspect Culture); *Factory Girls* (7:84 Theatre Company); *Variety, Decky does a Bronco* (Grid Iron); *Observe the Sons Of Ulster* (Citizens Theatre); *Romeo and Juliet* (Royal Lyceum Theatre, Edinburgh); *King Lear* (Royal Exchange, Manchester). Television work includes *Taggart* (SMG); *Real Men* (BBC).

John Kazek (*Frank*)
John trained at RSAMD. For the Traverse: *Gorgeous Avatar, I was
a Beautiful Day*, the *Slab Boys Trilogy, Solemn Mass for a Full Moon
in Summer* (Traverse/Barbican), *King of the Fields, Perfect Days*
(Traverse/Vaudeville), *Passing Places, Chic Nerds, Stones and Ashes,
Europe*. Other theatre includes *Fergus Lamont* (Communicado/Perth
Theatre); *Frozen* (Rapture Theatre); *Sea Change* (Oran Mor); *Cyrano
de Bergerac* (Catherine Wheels); *Roam* (Grid Iron/National Theatre
of Scotland); *1974 – The End of the Year Show* (Lyric Theatre,
Belfast); *Knives in Hens* (TAG Theatre Company); *Hedda Gabler,
Macbeth, Thebans, Uncle Vanya, 'Tis a Pity She's a Whore* (Theatre
Babel); *Word for Word* (Magnetic North); *Pleasure and Pain, Glue,
A Midsummer Night's Dream* (Citizens Theatre); *Marabou Stork
Nightmare* (Citizens Theatre/Leicester Haymarket Theatre); *Variety*
(Grid Iron); *The Big Funk* (The Arches); *Penetrator* (Tron Theatre);
Mary Queen of Scots, Kidnapped (Royal Lyceum Theatre, Edinburgh);
Twilight Shift (7:84 Theatre Company); *Wuthering Heights, Driving
Miss Daisy* (Byre Theatre); *King Lear, As You Like It* (Oxford Stage
Company). Television credits include *The Key* (BBC/Little Bird); *Auf
Wiedersehen Pet, City Central, Double Nougat, Rab C Nesbitt, Punch
Drunk, Strathblair* (BBC); *Taggart, High Road* (STV). Film credits
include *The Clan* (Clan Films); *Batman Begins* (Warner Bros); *Dear
Frankie* (Scorpio Films Ltd); *How D'Yae Want tae Die* (Dead Man's
Shoes Ltd); *Young Adam* (Hanway Films); *Riff Raff* (Parallax Pictures);
Silent Scream (Antonine Productions).

Kananu Kirimi (*Chris*)
Theatre credits include *The Soldier's Fortune* (Young Vic); *Romeo
& Juliet, The Tempest, Two Noble Kinsmen* (Shakespeare's Globe);
Paradise Lost (Bristol Old Vic); *A Doll's House* (Southwark Playhouse);
Fathers and Eggs (Company of Angels/Quicksilver Theatre); *The
Tempest, Pericles* (RSC); *Les Liaisons Dangereuses* (Liverpool Everyman
& Playhouse); *A Raisin in the Sun* (Young Vic/Salisbury Theatre);
Cinderella, Romeo & Juliet (Royal Lyceum Theatre, Edinburgh).
Television credits include *Sea of Souls* (Carnival Films); *Waking the
Dead* (BBC Drama Group); *The Royal* (ITV); *Ahead of the Class*
(World Productions/ARG TV); *Inspector Lynley, Rockface* (BBC);
The Deal (Granada); *Goodbye Mr Steadman* (Alibi Productions).
Film credits include *The Queen* (Granada Screen), *Trauma* (Trauma
Productions); *Small Love* (Tern TV); *Highlander: World Without End*
(Dimension Films).

Philip Pinsky (Composer)

Philip was a founder member of electro-acoustic group Finitribe, releasing five albums and performing over a period of 15 years. He now composes for film, theatre, TV and radio. In theatre he has composed scores for *Carthage Must Be Destroyed* (Traverse Theatre); *Once Upon a Dragon* (Grid Iron/Children's International Theatre Festival); *Roam* (Grid Iron/National Theatre of Scotland); *The Merchant of Venice, Faust 1 and 2* (Royal Lyceum Theatre, Edinburgh); *Fierce, The Houghmagandie Pack, Fermentation, Decky Does A Bronco* (Grid Iron); *Variety* (Edinburgh International Festival/Grid Iron); *A Chaste Maid In Cheapside, The Whizzkid, Ghost Ward* (Almeida Theatre); *DeoxyriboNucleic Acid* (Lyceum Youth Theatre/NT Connections); *Oedipus* (NTS Young Company); *The Man Who Was Thursday* (Red Shift Theatre Company). He was winner of the Critics Award for Theatre in Scotland 2005 for best use of music in theatre. Other work includes *Extraneous Noises Off* (BBC Radio 3, winner of Sony Radio Award), *Art and Soul* (BBC Scotland), *Ninewells* (BBC1), *Harley Street* (BBC1), education projects for the Scottish Chamber Orchestra and the signature music for MTV's European mobile phone channel. Philip is currently an Associate Artist at the Royal Lyceum Theatre, Edinburgh

Ros Steen (Voice Coach)

Ros trained at RSAMD and has worked extensively in theatre, film and TV. For the Traverse: *strangers, babies*, the *Tilt* triple bill, *Gorgeous Avatar, Melody, I was a Beautiful Day, East Coast Chicken Supper, The Found Man, In the Bag, Shimmer, The Nest*, the *Slab Boys Trilogy, Dark Earth, Homers, Outlying Islands, The Ballad of Crazy Paola, The Trestle at Pope Lick Creek, Heritage* (2001 and 1998), *Among Unbroken Hearts, Shetland Saga, Solemn Mass For a Full Moon in Summer* (as co-director) *King of the Fields, Highland Shorts, Family, Kill the Old Torture Their Young, Chic Nerds, Greta, Lazybed, Knives in Hens, Passing Places, Bondagers, Road to Nirvana, Sharp Shorts, Marisol, Grace in America*. Recent theatre credits include *The Bevellers, Shadow of a Gunman, No Mean City, Whatever Happened To Baby Jane?, Mystery of the Rose Bouquet* (Citizens Theatre); *Sweet Bird of Youth, The Talented Mr, Ripley, The Graduate, A Lie of the Mind* (Dundee Rep); *Black Watch, Mancub, Miss Julie* (National Theatre of Scotland); *The Wonderful World of Dissocia* (Edinburgh International Festival/Drum Theatre Plymouth/Tron Theatre), *The Rise and Fall of Little Voice* (Visible Fictions); *Perfect Pie* (Stellar Quines); *The Small Things* (Paines Plough); *My Mother Said I Never Should* (West Yorkshire Playhouse).

Film credits include *Greyfriars Bobby* (Piccadilly Pictures); *Gregory's Two Girls* (Channel Four Films). Television credits include *Sea of Souls, Rockface, 2000 Acres of Skye, Monarch of the Glen, Hamish Macbeth* (BBC).

Benny Young (*Bowman*) Recent theatre includes *Hughie, Tone Clusters* (Arches Theatre Company); *Jekyll and Hyde, Phèdre* (Perth Theatre); *As You Like It* (Royal Lyceum Theatre, Edinburgh); *The Importance of Being Alfred* (Oran Mor); *A Soldier's Tale* (Birmingham Symphony); *The Iceman Cometh* (The Old Vic); *Hosanna* (Tron Theatre); *Blood Wedding* (Communicado). Benny has also toured with The Touring Consortium in *The Crucible, A View From The Bridge* and *Hobson's Choice* and spent seasons with the Royal National Theatre, Royal Shakespeare Company, Royal Lyceum Theatre, Edinburgh and The Wrestling School. Television credits include *Waking The Dead: Sins of The Father, Spooks, Between the Lines* (BBC); *Talk To Me* (Company Pictures/ITV); *Taggart* (SMG); *The Bill* (Talkback Thames); *Doctor Finlay* (Scottish Television Enterprises); *Family Affairs* (Freemantle Media). Other television credits include two years as Brian Dunkley in *Coronation Street* and two years as DS Ted Hatchard in *Boon*. Film credits include *Chariots of Fire* (Warner Brothers Pictures); *Out of Africa* (Universal Pictures); *White Nights* (Columbia Pictures).

SPONSORSHIP AND DEVELOPMENT

We would like to thank the following
corporate funders for their support

B B C Scotland

LUMISON

HBJ Gateley Wareing

To find out how you can benefit
from being a Traverse Corporate Funder,
please contact our Development Department
on 0131 228 3223 / development@traverse.co.uk

The Traverse would like to thank
the members of the Development Board:

Ruth Allan, Adrienne Sinclair Chalmers, Stephen Cotton,
Roddy Martine, Paddy Scott and Teri Wishart

The Traverse Theatre's work
would not be possible without the support of

ARE YOU DEVOTED?

Our Devotees are:

Stewart Binnie, Katie Bradford, Adrienne Sinclair Chalmers, Adam Fowler, Anne Gallacher, Keith Guy, Helen Pitkethly, Michael Ridings

The Traverse could not function without the generous support of our patrons. In March 2006 the Traverse Devotees was launched to offer a whole host of exclusive benefits to our loyal supporters.

Become a Traverse Devotee for £28 per month or £350 per annum and receive:

- A night at the theatre including six tickets, drinks and a backstage tour

- Your name inscribed on a brick in our wall

- Sponsorship of one of our brand new Traverse 2 seats

- Invitations to Devotees' events

- Your name featured on this page in Traverse Theatre Company scripts and a copy mailed to you

- Free hire of the Traverse Bar Café (subject to availability)

Bricks in our wall and seats in Traverse 2 are also available separately. Inscribed with a message of your choice, these make ideal and unusual gifts.

To join the Devotees or to discuss giving us your support in another way, please contact our Development Department on 0131 228 3223 / development@traverse.co.uk

TRAVERSE THEATRE – THE COMPANY

NIGHT TIME

Selma Dimitrijević

for
Pamela Carter

Characters

CHRISTINA (CHRIS) BOWMAN, *thirties*
FRANK, *forties*
THOMAS, *late twenties*
BOWMAN, *Christina's husband, fifties*

A forward slash (/) indicates the point where the next speaker interrupts.

This text went to press before the end of rehearsals and so may differ slightly from the play as performed.

Scene One

There is an oversized white sofa in the middle of the stage.
Small side table next to it.

It's FRANK*'s house.*

CHRIS *enters.*

She shouldn't be there.

FRANK *enters.*

CHRIS	i'm really sorry.
FRANK	please.
CHRIS	thank you.
FRANK	it's alright.
CHRIS	i didn't mean to
FRANK	no. please. don't worry.
CHRIS	this is very . . . very kind of you.
FRANK	can i get you anything?
CHRIS	no. thank you.
FRANK	glass of water?
CHRIS	i'm sorry if i
FRANK	it's fine.
CHRIS	it's just . . . i don't want to – intrude.
FRANK	no. not at all.
CHRIS	and thank you. thank you for letting me in.
FRANK	of course.
CHRIS	it's just, if we stood there any longer you know someone might see us.
FRANK	no. you are right. absolutely right.

CHRIS	thank you.
FRANK	is there . . . would you like me to phone anyone? talk to someone.
CHRIS	actually, no. no, thank you.
FRANK	of course, you can phone, that's what i meant, if you'd like to call somebody.
CHRIS	i'd rather not. i'd have to – explain.
FRANK	i see.
CHRIS	no.
FRANK	sure. i understand.
CHRIS	and also, it's late. i think it's too late now. i'd better not.
FRANK	of course. if you think so.
CHRIS	i can't
FRANK	please. sit down. can i take your
CHRIS	thank you.

He helps her take her coat off.

Taking it off her shoulders is painful for her.

FRANK	it hurts?
CHRIS	no. well, yes. a bit.
FRANK	are you sure i can't get you anything?
CHRIS	i don't want to trouble you too much.
FRANK	not at all.
CHRIS	this is all very kind of you. it was getting cold outside.
FRANK	of course. you must be freezing.

CHRIS	it wasn't that bad.
FRANK	are you sure?
CHRIS	maybe a bit. it was wet and i think i walked around for a while.
FRANK	here.
	He hands her the blanket that was folded over the arm of the sofa.
	there you go.
CHRIS	thanks.
FRANK	that's better.
CHRIS	i wasn't sure if i should, you know, if i should knock, but i saw the lights. so i just thought
FRANK	of course you should. no, of course. i was just – reading. nothing else.
CHRIS	i know it's late.
FRANK	really. i was just i wasn't planning to go to bed. not any time soon.
CHRIS	i didn't want to wake anyone up.
FRANK	you didn't. it's just me.
CHRIS	oh good.
FRANK	did you . . . how long were you out there?
CHRIS	i don't know. not that long. maybe an hour. couple of hours.
FRANK	jesus, you must be freezing.
CHRIS	– i couldn't go back.
FRANK	no, of course not.
CHRIS	and i didn't know what else where else to go.

FRANK	no. you made a good . . . it's good.
CHRIS	thank you.
FRANK	–
CHRIS	–
FRANK	i was going to say
CHRIS	i won't stay long.
FRANK	no. i was going to ask you – do you have any place you could go to tonight?
CHRIS	a place i could go to?
FRANK	it is late. and i know it's hard, i mean – it must be hard, so . . . you'd be more than welcome to stay here.
CHRIS	oh, no. no.
FRANK	there's a spare room. and i really don't mind. you know, just in case you need a bit more time. to think. to clear your mind.
CHRIS	–
FRANK	you can think about it.
CHRIS	i don't know.
FRANK	well, the offer is there. just so you know. you don't need to worry about it right now.
CHRIS	i couldn't.
FRANK	if there's nowhere else
CHRIS	i shouldn't have come.
FRANK	that's not what i meant. i'm glad you came. i mean, obviously, it's awful. i didn't mean to say but if it had to be somewhere . . . i'm glad it's here.
CHRIS	you are?
FRANK	i live alone. it's warm. and safe. so you can

	but you don't have to stay. obviously. i won't mention it again. alright?
CHRIS	thank you.
FRANK	that's the least i can do.
CHRIS	seriously. that's very kind of you. to do this for someone you don't really know.
FRANK	not a complete stranger, are you?
CHRIS	almost.
FRANK	i know where you live.
CHRIS	yes, you must.
FRANK	well, that's a start.
CHRIS	i guess.
FRANK	i know we never talked or anything, but i'm just glad i can help. that's what neighbours are for, right?
CHRIS	i suppose.
FRANK	we were bound to meet sometime.
CHRIS	do you know my husband?
FRANK	no. i mean, i met him a couple of times.
CHRIS	have you?
FRANK	very briefly. just down the road.
CHRIS	did you talk?
FRANK	not much. he just says hello.
CHRIS	of course not.
FRANK	and so do i.
CHRIS	are you worried he / might
FRANK	no.
CHRIS	i'm not saying he would. i don't think he would but still.

FRANK	no one knows you're here.
CHRIS	when we were standing out at the front
FRANK	it was dark. there's nothing to worry about. i'm sure you can relax.
CHRIS	it was. i know. you're right.
FRANK	i really don't think you should go back tonight.
CHRIS	home?
FRANK	yes.
CHRIS	no. i can't.
FRANK	fine then.
CHRIS	but eventually
FRANK	yes?
CHRIS	i'll have to. i'll have to do something.
FRANK	i know. i know. but not just now. alright?
CHRIS	something else.
FRANK	don't worry about that now.
CHRIS	and i . . . i'm not sure what. i'm not sure what that will be.
FRANK	look . . . would you like me to call the police?
CHRIS	now?
FRANK	yes.
CHRIS	no. no. i don't think so. i don't think i want to talk to them right now.
FRANK	are you sure?
CHRIS	they might come.
FRANK	i could talk to them. if you want.
CHRIS	it's my fault.

FRANK	sorry?
CHRIS	all this, you know.
FRANK	no. don't say that. of course it's not.
CHRIS	that's what they'll say. it doesn't come as a not any more.
FRANK	why would they say something like that?

CHRIS	they do. every time. that's what they say. they
	    say they ask. but in fact they say.
	and it doesn't sound like a question. it never
	    does.

FRANK	i can't believe that. that's not right.
CHRIS	of course you can't. you are kind.
FRANK	but they don't have the right.
CHRIS	you let strangers into your house.
FRANK	stop saying you're a stranger.
CHRIS	we've never talked before.
FRANK	still.
CHRIS	i could be anyone.
FRANK	no.
CHRIS	and you still do all this.
FRANK	but i see you every day.
CHRIS	you do?
FRANK	well, maybe not every day.
CHRIS	how?
FRANK	you know, when you're coming in. or going out.
CHRIS	i don't go out.
FRANK	i just meant . . . i feel like i know you. it doesn't feel like you're a stranger.
CHRIS	no.

9

FRANK	that's all / i was
CHRIS	that's not what you were saying. is it?
FRANK	–
CHRIS	what did you mean by that?
FRANK	well, sometimes . . . sometimes i see you
CHRIS	yes?
FRANK	when you're walking by.
CHRIS	where?
FRANK	i can see your window. from upstairs. from mine.
CHRIS	my house?
FRANK	yes.
CHRIS	you can see inside?
FRANK	well, yes. when there's a light on. and when it's dark outside.
CHRIS	just like now?
FRANK	yes.
CHRIS	and you look?
FRANK	no. i wouldn't. well, yes. sometimes.
CHRIS	–
FRANK	just / when i
CHRIS	and what do you see?
FRANK	in the evening just every so often. i see you walking up and down. that's all.
CHRIS	you look at me.
FRANK	no. i can't sleep. it's not like i don't really look. i just notice you sometimes.

CHRIS	and
FRANK	–
CHRIS	am i on my own?
FRANK	sometimes you talk to someone.
CHRIS	my husband.
FRANK	could be. i wouldn't know. usually i don't see the other side.
CHRIS	there's no one else there.
FRANK	must be him then.
CHRIS	and you can see my bedroom?
FRANK	no. no. and even if i could. you know, i wouldn't look. you know, look.
CHRIS	but you do.
FRANK	you can't really help it.
CHRIS	so you see you see things that are private.
FRANK	no.
CHRIS	you must. did you ever see us / when
FRANK	no. i turn away. i walk out.
CHRIS	but would you tell me if you did?
FRANK	no. there's nothing. i don't see anything
CHRIS	not a thing?
FRANK	well, sometimes
CHRIS	yes?
FRANK	sometimes i see you take off your shirt, put your cream on that's all.
CHRIS	my cream?

FRANK	but i don't stay then. when i see that you are about to
	i leave.
CHRIS	why?
FRANK	it's not right.
CHRIS	and the rest of the time, you're thinking, what?
	–
	you know – is it ever right?
FRANK	i told you. i don't look for you.
	but if i'm standing by my window. having a cigarette. looking out.
	and i see your house. happen to see you just talking to someone.
	you know. there's no harm.
CHRIS	what else do you see?
FRANK	nothing.
CHRIS	so you never / saw him
FRANK	no.
	i told you.
CHRIS	but earlier
FRANK	it's true. i swear to you.
CHRIS	when i told you. just now.
	outside.
FRANK	i believed you.
CHRIS	you didn't ask any questions.
	you didn't seem surprised.
	you just let me in.
FRANK	i believed you. i take your word for
	but i've never seen it. or anything else. no.
	i mean, there's no reason to doubt.
CHRIS	so you just let me in. without a question.
FRANK	of course.
CHRIS	don't you think that's

FRANK	you needed to get out of the cold. it's not much. and someone to talk to. really not that much. and if i can help
CHRIS	you were more than happy to.
FRANK	i didn't mind. i really don't mind.
CHRIS	were you expecting me?
FRANK	no. of course not.
CHRIS	but
FRANK	what?
CHRIS	were you thinking one day i might come?
FRANK	–
CHRIS	were you?
FRANK	no.
CHRIS	but now that i'm here.
FRANK	i'm just glad i can help.
CHRIS	–
FRANK	look. if there was anything wrong with it, if i felt it was wrong i'd never tell you.
CHRIS	why did you tell me?
FRANK	i don't know, i thought you might feel better, more comfortable, if you knew that we know each other.
CHRIS	but we don't.
FRANK	i thought it might help.
CHRIS	maybe i should go now.
FRANK	look
CHRIS	i should.
FRANK	you can't.

CHRIS	i'm sorry?
FRANK	i mean, it's better if you don't.
CHRIS	you can't stop me.
FRANK	where will you go?
CHRIS	it doesn't matter.
FRANK	it does.
CHRIS	home.
FRANK	you can't. you're safer here.
CHRIS	safer than what?
FRANK	that's not what i meant.
CHRIS	why did you let me in?
FRANK	you looked like you needed a friend.
CHRIS	we are not friends.
FRANK	maybe not friends
CHRIS	you don't know me.
FRANK	i feel like i do.
CHRIS	do you?
FRANK	sometimes.
CHRIS	and that's why you let me in?
FRANK	no. it has nothing to do with it.
CHRIS	with the fact that you look at me?
FRANK	i'd do it anyway.
CHRIS	would you?
FRANK	of course i would.
CHRIS	just let anyone into your house?
FRANK	if they need help. yes. of course i would.

CHRIS	and if you never saw me before? if you had no idea who i was?
FRANK	look
CHRIS	just a strange woman coming to your door.
FRANK	i would.
CHRIS	you know it? you are absolutely certain you would let anyone in?
FRANK	i don't know. maybe not anyone.
CHRIS	so you don't know?
FRANK	i don't. alright? to be honest, i think i would. that's all i can say.
CHRIS	and what if it was a man?
FRANK	a man?
CHRIS	if a man showed up at your door?
FRANK	what does that have to do with anything?
CHRIS	a man came to your door.
FRANK	he didn't.
CHRIS	i know. i did.
FRANK	but you're not a man.
CHRIS	would you do this if i was?
FRANK	talk to you?
CHRIS	let me into your home?
FRANK	i don't know. maybe. i suppose i would. depends.
CHRIS	on what?
FRANK	the situation.
CHRIS	i come to your door. same as now. but i'm a man. and i haven't been invited.
FRANK	alright.

CHRIS	can you imagine it?

FRANK   i can.

CHRIS   can you?

FRANK   how old is he?

CHRIS   about your age.

FRANK   unhurt?

CHRIS   on the surface. yes.

FRANK   is he asking to come in?

CHRIS   no.
just standing there.
looking at you.
looking up. at him.

FRANK   alright.

CHRIS   so?

FRANK   the truth?

CHRIS   yes.

FRANK   i don't know.

CHRIS   of course you do.

FRANK   i'm trying to be honest with you. that's all i . . .
    that's all i can do.

    –

this is not fair.

CHRIS   it's just a question.

FRANK   that's all i can say. i really don't know.
look. i was just trying to help you. of course
    you can leave if you want to.
i don't know what you – i don't know enough.
and i know there's not much i can do.
but if there's anything, anything at all.
i would do it for anyone.

CHRIS   –

you mean that, don't you?

FRANK	i do.
CHRIS	and you are nothing like him. you would never do anything like that?
FRANK	of course not.
CHRIS	you sound so sure.
FRANK	i am. i'm absolutely sure.
CHRIS	how can you be?
FRANK	i don't know. that's one thing i just am.
CHRIS	but you still look.
FRANK	it's not the same. it's nothing like . . . no. no.
CHRIS	and if if i wasn't here? right now. would you be looking at me now?
FRANK	–
CHRIS	–
FRANK	i don't know. maybe.
CHRIS	and you do it every night?
FRANK	no.
CHRIS	but often enough.
FRANK	i see how it sounds.
CHRIS	and do you imagine things? before you see me? while you're waiting?
FRANK	it's not like that. i told you. it just happens. sometimes i just look up and see you walking up and down.
CHRIS	don't you get bored?

FRANK	it's not like that. it's usually just a moment. when you're passing by, and when i'm passing by.
CHRIS	and i never knew.
FRANK	there's nothing to it.
CHRIS	you think?
FRANK	nothing.
CHRIS	so i shouldn't mind? i shouldn't feel like / you're
FRANK	look
CHRIS	and do you think if your girlfriend knew, you think she wouldn't mind?
FRANK	my girlfriend?
CHRIS	yes.
FRANK	there is no – i don't have a girlfriend.
CHRIS	a partner.
FRANK	no. no one.
CHRIS	you must have someone.
FRANK	no. i don't. not now.
CHRIS	but there was someone.
FRANK	yes.
CHRIS	someone who might have minded you looking / at me.
FRANK	she wouldn't mind.
CHRIS	is that why she left?
FRANK	no. how can you it was something else. and she left. alright?

CHRIS	why?
FRANK	– i don't know.
CHRIS	you must.
FRANK	i don't.
CHRIS	so where is she now?
FRANK	at her new house. i suppose.
CHRIS	do you still see her? do you ever go to
FRANK	no. she's not alone. i don't think i'd be it's not my place.
CHRIS	new partner?
FRANK	a husband this time.
CHRIS	oh.
FRANK	yes.
CHRIS	and you don't worry?
FRANK	about her?
CHRIS	yes. about him. what he's like.
FRANK	he seems nice enough. she says he is. and i'm sure she's right. i have to believe her. she's pretty smart.
CHRIS	and he would never do anything like that?
FRANK	no. never.
CHRIS	you see, that's what people usually say.
FRANK	he wouldn't.
CHRIS	so what would you do?
FRANK	when?
CHRIS	if he did. if it happened to her.
FRANK	i really hope it doesn't.

CHRIS	your hope won't help her much.
FRANK	i know. it's just
CHRIS	what would you do?
FRANK	i don't know. try to make it better, i suppose.
CHRIS	how?
FRANK	ask her.
CHRIS	ask her what?
FRANK	ask her about it. if i can.
CHRIS	you think she would want to talk?

FRANK	she would. she always did. if anything
	    happened – that's the one thing we could
	    always do. we could always talk.

CHRIS	and if she doesn't want to?
FRANK	i wouldn't insist.
CHRIS	no?
FRANK	never.
CHRIS	alright. so she talks.
FRANK	i'd listen. and try to understand. i don't think i could. for someone like me that's – but i would try.
CHRIS	understand him? or her?
FRANK	the whole situation. her. what she must be feeling. what she might be needing. offer help. i don't know. if there was anything anything i might do – anything she might need.
CHRIS	is that so?
FRANK	yes.
CHRIS	a bit like now?
FRANK	maybe. yes.

CHRIS	but what could you tell her?
FRANK	that she's not on her own. that i'm there.
CHRIS	that you are 'there'?
FRANK	for her.
CHRIS	i see. and you are there to do what – exactly?
FRANK	to do whatever she needs me to do.
CHRIS	so you presume she needs you?
FRANK	i don't.
CHRIS	yes you do.
FRANK	look, this is not my fault. what happened to / you is

CHRIS	i was asking about her.
	    –
	you would take her back. wouldn't you? ask
	    her in.

FRANK	yes. do whatever i can.
CHRIS	help her.
FRANK	yes. find out if she needs any money.
CHRIS	she might be offended.

FRANK	she wouldn't be. it would be a loan. she would
	    know that. i don't have much anyway. i could
	    offer some for a ticket.

CHRIS	a ticket?
FRANK	in case she wants to leave town. a train ticket maybe. or a bus fare.
CHRIS	and what happens if she needs more?
FRANK	more than what?
CHRIS	to go further.

FRANK	i don't know. i can't give her much more.
CHRIS	that's true.
FRANK	but i could drive her somewhere. if she needs to. she could use my phone. or a bed.
CHRIS	in the spare room?
FRANK	yes, she could sleep here. rest. stay for a while. as long as she needs to.
CHRIS	with you?
FRANK	at my house.
CHRIS	do you think she would want that?
FRANK	i don't know. i would ask her. i wouldn't do anything without asking her. never. trust me.
CHRIS	would you help with her cuts?
FRANK	what cuts?
CHRIS	there are cuts.
FRANK	no.
CHRIS	there are.
FRANK	what kind of cuts?
CHRIS	small. deep. some of them are.
FRANK	–
CHRIS	–
FRANK	i would. of course i would.
CHRIS	would you know how to?
FRANK	i've done it before.
CHRIS	how come?
FRANK	at work.
CHRIS	you deal with wounds at work?

FRANK	sometimes. yes.
CHRIS	what do you do?
FRANK	let's say . . . i help people.
CHRIS	how?
FRANK	if something happened to them. if they were . . . unfortunate.
CHRIS	where?
FRANK	if they were sleeping rough. for example. if they are cold. or hungry.
CHRIS	or hurt.
FRANK	yes. some of them are.
CHRIS	and you help them.
FRANK	if i can.
CHRIS	are you
FRANK	what?
CHRIS	are you making this up?
FRANK	no.
CHRIS	–
FRANK	i'm not.
CHRIS	it's all very convenient. are you sure you are not just making it up? imagining. and telling me
FRANK	why would i do that?
CHRIS	to make me feel safe.
FRANK	you are safe here.
CHRIS	–
FRANK	–
CHRIS	so you think you could you would dress her cuts?

FRANK	i'd try. i'd do whatever i can.
CHRIS	she would be grateful.
FRANK	it's not much.
CHRIS	so when it happens to her
FRANK	it won't.
CHRIS	well, i don't know that. and neither do you. how could we? she's away now.
FRANK	no one would do that to her.
CHRIS	and if someone did, you wouldn't be able to stop it.
FRANK	maybe.
CHRIS	no. you wouldn't.
FRANK	it would never happen – she's not
CHRIS	yes?
FRANK	it doesn't matter.
CHRIS	you were going to say it would never happen to her. weren't you? and why is that? because she is 'pretty smart'?
FRANK	so are you.
CHRIS	you were going to say she is not that type.
FRANK	i wasn't.
CHRIS	you thought it.
FRANK	–
CHRIS	you did.
FRANK	yes, i did.
CHRIS	but you weren't going to say it.
FRANK	no.

CHRIS	what stopped you?
FRANK	i didn't want to hurt you.
CHRIS	you thought it.
FRANK	i'm really sorry.
CHRIS	don't apologise. you don't decide what / you
FRANK	i mean it. it's a stupid thing to think. i know. and i don't even think that. i didn't mean it like that.
CHRIS	– you are a very kind man, Frank. you know that, don't you?
FRANK	i'm sorry.
CHRIS	and it can happen to anyone.
FRANK	i know.
CHRIS	even to her.
FRANK	i just want to protect her.
CHRIS	i know.
FRANK	she was angry. when i saw her last. she was – hurt.
CHRIS	was that you?
FRANK	no. not like that. i'd never but you know that by now.
CHRIS	i do.
FRANK	it's just
CHRIS	what happened?
FRANK	i don't know what i was a fool.
CHRIS	do you you think you hurt her?
FRANK	i might have.

CHRIS	how?
FRANK	i don't know how.
CHRIS	but you know you did?
FRANK	it wasn't nice.
CHRIS	how?
FRANK	i would talk to her this time.
CHRIS	would you know what to say?
FRANK	–
CHRIS	would you ask her to sit with you?
FRANK	–
CHRIS	would you hold her?
FRANK	i would.
CHRIS	but she is someone's wife.
FRANK	– i'd take her hand.
CHRIS	her hand?
FRANK	yes. if she'd let me.
CHRIS	she might.
FRANK	just to talk to her. just talk.
CHRIS	what would you say? what would you ask?
FRANK	i'd have to say sorry.
CHRIS	what for?
FRANK	for earlier.
CHRIS	when she was here?
FRANK	it was harsh.
CHRIS	what was?
FRANK	i was.

CHRIS	just once?
FRANK	no.
CHRIS	twice?
FRANK	i'm sorry. i'd have to say that. i'd have to apologise.
CHRIS	would she believe you?
FRANK	it was stupid. a stupid thing to do.
	–
	but i never hit her. i never touched her that way.
CHRIS	–
FRANK	do you believe me?
CHRIS	was she scared?
FRANK	no. she was never scared. it wasn't like that. i wouldn't do that. i was just stupid. just things i said. i knew what to say. what would hurt.
CHRIS	and now you would
FRANK	apologise.
CHRIS	to her.
FRANK	i'm sorry.
CHRIS	–
FRANK	i really didn't mean to. didn't mean to say those things.
CHRIS	i know.
FRANK	do you believe me?
CHRIS	i do.
FRANK	you're safe here.
CHRIS	you don't have to say that.
FRANK	and you can stay here tonight.
CHRIS	i can't.

FRANK   of course you can.

CHRIS   no. i'm sorry.

FRANK   –

CHRIS   not this time.

FRANK   why?

CHRIS   do you have to ask?

FRANK   it would be

CHRIS   it would be easy to do it.
i know.

FRANK   it would.

CHRIS   like every other time.

FRANK   –

CHRIS   but i can't. i have to say no. and it's not . . . but
i can't.
can you understand that?
it's not that simple.
people would find out. you know what it's like.
sooner or later someone would notice. and they
would find out.
and what would you do then? what would you
tell them?

FRANK   it's not like that.

CHRIS   no?
what would you say?
it's not how it seems? it's different with you?
it just happened once. twice?
it's different this time?
or
it wasn't what you intended to do?
you didn't mean to? it's not how it sounds?
do *you* hear how it sounds?
–
and they might believe you. who knows.
people hear what they want to hear.
they don't ask.

	they want to know if you're doing 'fine'. and
	you say you're fine.

they want to know if you're doing 'fine'. and
    you say you're fine.
i'm fine.
i'm fine.
you say it enough times
and somehow that makes it all alright.

FRANK   Chris.

CHRIS   and even if they see it, you see, if somehow
    they see us, there's always an explanation. it
    can't be, it can't be how it looks. they catch
    a glimpse. overhear a conversation. even just
    a line – and it's too late, they've made up
    their minds. we can say nothing happened,
    but people see what they want to see, and it
    doesn't matter, doesn't matter what you say
    after that, or how many times you repeat it,
    you can keep repeating it until you bleed out.

FRANK   –

CHRIS   just a happy couple.
    that's all they want to hear.
    it gives them hope. it says the whole thing is
        possible.
    somehow.
    that's what they need to believe. it makes it
        easier for them.
    doesn't matter what i say.

    you say i worry too much. and you say it like i
        shouldn't. you say there's nothing to worry
        about. and what we know is just between us.
        it's ours.
    like it's a good thing to have.
    no one else knows. just you and i.
    and sometimes we pretend that even we don't
        know.
    it makes it easier.
    maybe we can even forget all about it. forget it
        happened.
    you see, if only we know, and we forget, who
        can say it ever happened?

after all, you say, it's just us. nothing big.
    nothing important, my dear.
just us.

but i can't.
and i don't know if you actually hear it.
if the words come out.
i say i can't, you say of course you can.
it doesn't take much effort. just stay, stay here
    with me.
it's not that hard.
don't have to move.
don't have to decide.
relax.
stay just one more night.
go to your bed.
we'll talk in the morning.
think about everything some other time.
things might be different this time.
you say
it's nice. it's warm. it's safe. it could be fun.
it doesn't matter if you're tired. if you're feeling
    numb.
it's me. stay.
staying doesn't demand any effort.
and you can always do the thinking some other
    time.
but i thought about it.
i had enough time.
it's too late now.

i can't. not this time.

She turns around. FRANK *is not there any
more.*

She is on her own.

Scene Two

Same sofa, same blanket.

This is now THOMAS*'s flat.*

THOMAS *enters with two coffees.*

Puts them on the table. Sits down.

CHRIS *is in the background, looking at him for a moment or two.*

He seems very comfortable on his own.

She is observing him for a while.

CHRIS   hey.

               He turns around.

THOMAS   hi there.

CHRIS   good morning.

THOMAS   morning.

               She comes closer.

               how are you?

CHRIS   fine.

THOMAS   coffee?

CHRIS   thank you.

               CHRIS *takes it.*

               Takes a sip.

               what time is it?

THOMAS   almost five.

CHRIS   in the morning?

THOMAS   yes.

CHRIS	it's so bright outside.
THOMAS	short nights.
	She smiles.
	what?
CHRIS	i can't remember the last time i was up at this time.
THOMAS	go back to bed.
CHRIS	no, it's fine.
THOMAS	really, you don't have to stay up.
CHRIS	well, i woke up and you know, you weren't there, so i thought
THOMAS	i was making coffee.
CHRIS	of course.
THOMAS	it's not the real coffee. i'm sorry. just . . . cheap stuff.
CHRIS	no. it's good. delicious actually.
THOMAS	well, thank you.
CHRIS	i haven't had it for a while.
THOMAS	so . . . did you sleep alright?
CHRIS	yes, i did.
THOMAS	good.
CHRIS	i did.
THOMAS	you didn't sleep much.
CHRIS	i don't know. maybe i woke up a couple of times.
THOMAS	i'm sorry.
CHRIS	no. it wasn't you.
THOMAS	the thing is, you get so used to sleeping on your own and not . . . you know, not with . . . someone.

CHRIS	really, it wasn't you.
THOMAS	was it the street?
CHRIS	i don't think so.
THOMAS	it can be noisy around here, you know, people get up to all sorts of things during the night.
CHRIS	i didn't really hear them.
THOMAS	no. neither did i. but, you know. sometimes you do. some people do. sometimes.
CHRIS	i'm sure they do.
THOMAS	– kind of stating the obvious.
CHRIS	that's fine.
THOMAS	sorry. i'll try not to.

She gets more comfortable on the sofa.

CHRIS	so is this
THOMAS	yes?
CHRIS	is this something you do often? you know, get up at this time?
THOMAS	i guess. you know, if the sun is out.
CHRIS	and what do you do? i mean . . . what do you do with all that time?
THOMAS	oh, i don't know. not much. sit here. chill out. enjoy my coffee for a while.
CHRIS	chill out?
THOMAS	yes.
CHRIS	just like that. on your own?
THOMAS	most of the time. i mean, i don't have a habit of bringing people / back to my
CHRIS	no. no. i didn't mean it like that. god no.

33

THOMAS	it's ok. you're here. you have the right to ask. and no, i don't
CHRIS	no. none of my business.
THOMAS	and how about you?
CHRIS	what do i do in the morning?
THOMAS	okay. yes.
CHRIS	i don't know. same i guess. just not as early. in fact i usually have tea. most days. first i have a cup of tea.
THOMAS	on your own?
CHRIS	no.
THOMAS	oh.
CHRIS	yes.
THOMAS	with your . . . ?
CHRIS	husband.
THOMAS	right.
CHRIS	yes.
THOMAS	well, you know . . . it happens.
CHRIS	it does.

She puts the blanket over her feet.

	and how about you? do you have anyone?
THOMAS	no. not at the moment. well . . . i don't think i do.
CHRIS	you don't think you do?
THOMAS	well, yes.
CHRIS	but how can you . . . how can you not know?
THOMAS	you know how it is.
CHRIS	i don't.
THOMAS	basically it's up to me. i'm not sure what's really going on. i just need to decide.

CHRIS	right. that's interesting.
THOMAS	it's not bad.
CHRIS	well, good for you then –

Trying to remember his name.

THOMAS	Thomas.
CHRIS	Thomas. of course.
THOMAS	yes.
CHRIS	i would have got it.
THOMAS	it's fine.
CHRIS	i'm Chris.
THOMAS	yes. you said. hi.
CHRIS	that's terrible. i'm sorry.
THOMAS	don't be.
CHRIS	i'm really sorry i forgot your name.
THOMAS	maybe i didn't mention it.
CHRIS	no, you did. last night. i just wasn't paying attention.
	that is terrible. sorry about that.
THOMAS	well, it happens. people forget stuff.
CHRIS	it shouldn't. i won't forget it now.
THOMAS	should i write it down?
CHRIS	that won't be necessary.
THOMAS	i could wear a badge.
CHRIS	stop it.
THOMAS	–
	i'm glad you came though. and . . . i'm really glad you didn't have to leave last night.
CHRIS	i know. so am i.

She takes another sip of coffee.

THOMAS	i was going to let you sleep, just now. you must be tired.
CHRIS	no. not at all. i dropped off quite quickly last night.
	as soon as . . . i was out.
THOMAS	you were?
CHRIS	just like that.
THOMAS	right.
CHRIS	what?
THOMAS	are you sure?
CHRIS	why?
THOMAS	you stayed awake for quite a while.
CHRIS	no.
THOMAS	i could feel the difference.
CHRIS	–
THOMAS	you were close to me, and when you finally fell asleep . . . i could feel you, i could feel your body relax into mine.
CHRIS	you could?
THOMAS	it was almost dawn.
CHRIS	i'm sorry.
THOMAS	no reason to be.
CHRIS	look. i didn't want to pretend, you know, to be asleep. i wasn't trying to . . .
THOMAS	you don't have to apologise. actually it was / kind of
CHRIS	i wasn't
THOMAS	hey.
CHRIS	–
THOMAS	i was going to say it was kind of nice. alright?

CHRIS   alright.

THOMAS   good.

CHRIS   good.

THOMAS   so, tell me. what was it? too tired to sleep?

CHRIS   i guess, the whole day really was a bit of a . . .
                 and a hard night.
             i don't know. i guess i just needed some head
                 space. some time.

THOMAS   to be on your own?

CHRIS   yes.

THOMAS   and then i show up.

CHRIS   no. it's not like that.
             really. it was good to talk.
             i just needed to be away from
             well, i just needed to think. to clear my mind.

THOMAS   and. did it work?

CHRIS   i don't know yet. maybe.
             but . . . you helped. you really did.
             you don't know how much.
             –
             and i had a good time.

THOMAS   you did?

CHRIS   of course i did.

THOMAS   very good.

CHRIS   do you think it was a stupid thing to do?

THOMAS   what? have a good time?

CHRIS   no.
             you know . . .

THOMAS   what?

CHRIS   for me to come up?

THOMAS   fuck no. i mean, no, not at all.

CHRIS   but i didn't know you.

THOMAS	listen, it wasn't that kind of invitation.
CHRIS	i didn't know that either.
THOMAS	come on, you must have. we talked for hours.
CHRIS	well, maybe an hour.
THOMAS	did i make you come up?
CHRIS	no.
THOMAS	did you force your way in?
CHRIS	no.
THOMAS	well, there you go. we talked. we had a glass of wine. you had a good time. that's allowed.
CHRIS	i was just worried
THOMAS	you worry far too much.
CHRIS	the thing is . . . i think i've upset someone. when i came here. last night.
THOMAS	oh. your husband?
CHRIS	no. no. someone else. a really nice guy. you know . . . very decent. very honest kind of guy.
THOMAS	so there is someone else?
CHRIS	no. just a friend. someone i . . . actually, i just met him last night.
THOMAS	wow. busy night.
CHRIS	it wasn't like that.
THOMAS	i was just joking. sorry. bad joke. tell me. what happened?

CHRIS	i'm not sure.
	we were just talking and . . . and something
	    wasn't right.
	you know, how i thought it would be. i just
	    needed a bit of
	so, yes. i had to stop it. i had to get out of there.

38

THOMAS	he didn't try anything?
CHRIS	no. it wasn't like that. just a misunderstanding. i think we were both a bit tired. he was telling me about his anyway, it just wasn't right. so i left. and that's how i ended up waiting for the train.
THOMAS	the train?
CHRIS	yes. well, i didn't go anywhere. obviously. but that's why i was there. i told you, i was going home. to my parents' house actually. but then –
THOMAS	then?
CHRIS	well, then i met you.
THOMAS	oh, yes. yes, of course. then you met me.
CHRIS	and you never made it to your friend's.
THOMAS	my friend's?
CHRIS	were you not going to see / one of your
THOMAS	oh, last night?
CHRIS	yes. last night.

THOMAS	right. yes. i was. that's true. but it wasn't
	    anything important. i just haven't seen him
	    for a while.

CHRIS	so just to say hi.
THOMAS	that's right.
CHRIS	right.
THOMAS	what?
CHRIS	at one in the morning?
THOMAS	no. it wasn't that late. was it?
CHRIS	it was. quarter to one. i was waiting for the last train.

THOMAS	that's funny. i guess i just didn't realise how . . . how late it was.
CHRIS	and he won't be surprised you didn't show up?
THOMAS	i don't think so. i think he's quite used to it by now.
CHRIS	right.
THOMAS	yes.
CHRIS	can i ask you something?
THOMAS	go on.
CHRIS	are you making this up?
THOMAS	what?
CHRIS	all this. about your friend. are you making it up?
THOMAS	no. why would i?
CHRIS	what were you actually doing there in the middle of the night?
THOMAS	listen
CHRIS	were you waiting for somebody?
THOMAS	no.
CHRIS	were you going somewhere?
THOMAS	no.
CHRIS	well, what else would you be doing there at one in the morning? you don't go to a place like that just to stand there on your own.
THOMAS	fuck.
CHRIS	what is it?
THOMAS	i really like you, you know.
CHRIS	and?
THOMAS	and i don't want to scare you.
CHRIS	why would you do that?

THOMAS	it's nothing big.
CHRIS	what were you doing there?
THOMAS	i can't tell you.
CHRIS	you won't tell me?
THOMAS	no. i can't.
CHRIS	i'm just you asking you / a simple
THOMAS	hey.
CHRIS	you said i can ask. now you say i can't.
THOMAS	it's not like that.
CHRIS	then tell me.
THOMAS	i would love to. but i just don't know right now.
CHRIS	what do you mean you don't know?
THOMAS	i don't remember.
CHRIS	you don't remember?
THOMAS	no. i don't.
CHRIS	what is it that you don't remember?
THOMAS	last night.
CHRIS	you forgot what happened last night?
THOMAS	yes.
CHRIS	all of it?
THOMAS	most of it.
CHRIS	and how's that possible?
THOMAS	i know how it sounds. it's . . . fuck. i'd really like to tell you but i just, i just don't know now. at the moment. i don't remember.
CHRIS	let me get this straight. you went out in the middle of the night. you know you were at the train station. but you can't remember exactly why?

THOMAS	yes, that's right. well, not really. i can't remember i was there either.
CHRIS	at all?
THOMAS	that's right.
CHRIS	and the fact that we met there?
THOMAS	i've just found that out.
CHRIS	from me telling you? just now?
THOMAS	yes.
CHRIS	and you didn't think to mention it before?
THOMAS	i didn't want to scare you.
CHRIS	i'm not scared.
THOMAS	good.
CHRIS	so . . . what do you remember?
THOMAS	from last night?
CHRIS	yes.
THOMAS	not much.
CHRIS	were you drunk?
THOMAS	no. nothing like that.
CHRIS	then how can you tell me, i mean . . . how can you know that . . . i'm sorry. i don't understand.
THOMAS	it just happens sometimes.
CHRIS	just happens.
THOMAS	it does.
CHRIS	how often?
THOMAS	listen, i forget stuff. it's not a big deal. it doesn't influence my . . . you know, not much.
CHRIS	so the fact that this morning . . . that i was sleeping next to you . . . that i was there, in your bed?

THOMAS	complete fucking surprise.
CHRIS	you must be joking.
THOMAS	but obviously a very nice surprise.
CHRIS	Thomas.
THOMAS	i'm not being funny. and i'm not making it up. i swear to you. i just forget stuff.
CHRIS	you should be scared then, not i.
THOMAS	well, i got rather used to it by now.
CHRIS	right.
THOMAS	i know how it sounds.
CHRIS	so you woke up this morning and?
THOMAS	actually, i never fell asleep.
CHRIS	at all?
THOMAS	i don't think so. maybe for a few minutes.
CHRIS	but you can't be sure?
THOMAS	okay. what i do remember is . . . i remember trying not to fall asleep. i liked being next to . . . you know, i liked you. and talking to you. you seemed different. and it was nice. and i thought if i fall asleep i'll probably forget it all and when i wake up . . . you won't be there to remind me. so i thought if i can try and not, you know, fall asleep . . . all night.
CHRIS	but?
THOMAS	but then, you see, i'm not so sure. i was making coffee this morning. and it felt good. you know, for two. i know that much. but i couldn't really remember who you are. so i just figured . . . i must have fallen asleep after all. maybe just for a moment. and i knew . . . i just have to give it a bit of time and . . . i'll find out.

CHRIS	you mean i'll tell you?
THOMAS	well, yes.
CHRIS	Thomas.
THOMAS	sorry. i should've told you.
CHRIS	so you don't recall anything from last night?
THOMAS	not really.
CHRIS	and things i told you?
THOMAS	you can tell me again.
CHRIS	it wasn't anything . . . we didn't talk about that much.
THOMAS	we didn't have sex either.
CHRIS	no.
THOMAS	i know. you still had your shirt on. when i woke up. i mean, not that it means anything.
CHRIS	we didn't. no. we talked for a bit. about . . . things. it was fun. we laughed.
THOMAS	that sounds about right.
CHRIS	yes. you were funny.
THOMAS	that would be me.
CHRIS	and then you started taking your clothes off . . .
THOMAS	i did what?
CHRIS	well, first it was just the t-shirt. you said you have something to show me.
THOMAS	no.
CHRIS	then you undid your trousers . . .
THOMAS	fuck. why didn't you stop me?
CHRIS	you just wouldn't listen.
THOMAS	what a fucking idiot. listen, i'm so sorry.

CHRIS *starts laughing.*

what?

CHRIS   what?

THOMAS   you . . .
               are you messing with me?
               did you just make that up?

CHRIS   kind of.

THOMAS   oh. that's mean.

CHRIS   i couldn't resist.

THOMAS   you're a mean, mean woman, you know that?

CHRIS   i'm sorry.

THOMAS   you just wait until
               what's that?

CHRIS   what?

THOMAS   is that blood?

CHRIS   oh, god.

THOMAS   is it blood?

CHRIS   just a scratch.

THOMAS   a cut.

CHRIS   it's nothing. really.

THOMAS   will you just let me . . . what happened?

CHRIS   nothing.

THOMAS   did you just cut yourself?

CHRIS   no. it's old. from last night.

THOMAS   we should put something on it.

CHRIS   no. it's fine. it happened before.
               it's fine.

THOMAS   it's not fine.

CHRIS   really. it's fine.

THOMAS	alright.
CHRIS	so, tell me . . .
THOMAS	are you sure?
CHRIS	yes, tell me, you really don't remember what happened last night?
THOMAS	no.
CHRIS	and when i leave
THOMAS	you're not going now?
CHRIS	when i leave, you might not remember me at all. that i was here.
THOMAS	i might for a while.
CHRIS	and then?
THOMAS	it will all disappear.
CHRIS	and everything we talked about?
THOMAS	you can always tell me again.
CHRIS	but if i don't. you'll forget all of it, won't you?
THOMAS	yes. unless you come back. and if we talk again. then things stay with me.
CHRIS	but if we don't see each other again?
THOMAS	it will be as if we never met.
CHRIS	it will be what, like a dream?
THOMAS	no. i'd remember a dream. same as with you.
CHRIS	and you won't remember last night? or this morning? me? anything we talked about?
THOMAS	but we can talk now. you can remind me what we talked about last night.
CHRIS	it wasn't anything important.
THOMAS	it might have been.
CHRIS	no.

THOMAS	i think it was.
CHRIS	–
THOMAS	it was, wasn't it?
CHRIS	and how would you know?
THOMAS	was it about your friend?
CHRIS	it wasn't about him.
THOMAS	someone else?
CHRIS	we didn't really talk that much.
THOMAS	you were upset.
CHRIS	how would you know? you're just guessing now.
THOMAS	i think you were. you were worried.
CHRIS	–
THOMAS	weren't you?
CHRIS	yes. i was.
THOMAS	what about?
CHRIS	it doesn't matter now.
THOMAS	was it about me?
CHRIS	no.
THOMAS	when i invited you to come up
CHRIS	no. i liked that. you didn't seem to expect
THOMAS	i told you. i don't expect anything. i've learned that much.
CHRIS	i know. and that was nice.
THOMAS	tell me, what was it?
CHRIS	–
THOMAS	–
CHRIS	i had something to think about. that's why i was there. at the station. i had to clear my mind.

THOMAS	okay. and?
CHRIS	i didn't want to go home. but obviously i couldn't stay out all night.
THOMAS	and your friend?
CHRIS	no. i couldn't go back to him. and i didn't want to.
THOMAS	what about your husband?
CHRIS	what about him?
THOMAS	wasn't he waiting for you?
CHRIS	maybe.
THOMAS	he didn't know you left?
CHRIS	i'm sure he noticed.
THOMAS	you didn't talk to him?
CHRIS	no.
THOMAS	and you don't want to now?
CHRIS	no.
THOMAS	won't he be worried?
CHRIS	he will. but it's too late now.
THOMAS	things you had to think about . . . was that about him?
CHRIS	you'll forget it all anyway.
THOMAS	exactly. so you have nothing to lose.
CHRIS	and what do you get from knowing it?
THOMAS	at least i'll know it for a while.
CHRIS	–
THOMAS	–
CHRIS	i left my husband.
THOMAS	you did?

CHRIS	yes.
THOMAS	when?
CHRIS	last night.
THOMAS	wow.
CHRIS	do you believe me?
THOMAS	of course i do. why wouldn't i?
CHRIS	because i'm not going back.
THOMAS	alright.
CHRIS	i'm going to see my parents. and i can stay there. at least for a while.
THOMAS	listen.
CHRIS	you don't believe me?
THOMAS	i do. of course i do. it's just . . .
CHRIS	what?
THOMAS	i hope you won't be sorry. that's all. it's not a small thing.
CHRIS	that's funny.
THOMAS	why is that funny?
CHRIS	that's exactly what you said last night.
THOMAS	when you told me . . . ?
CHRIS	yes, when i told you for the first time.
THOMAS	fuck. sorry about that.
CHRIS	no. it's good. it's good to know you don't change your mind.
THOMAS	what else did i say?
CHRIS	actually, you were very nice.
THOMAS	thank you very much.
CHRIS	seriously, you were. like you understood.
THOMAS	it can't be easy being on your own.

CHRIS	like you've been through . . . something similar.
THOMAS	i might have. but then again, i wouldn't know, would i?
CHRIS	i think you have.
THOMAS	why do you say that?
CHRIS	i don't know. just the things you said. and how. you knew what to do. and you asked me back here. very gently. very gentlemanly.
THOMAS	and you said yes.
CHRIS	i did.
THOMAS	i'm glad you did. i was hoping last night . . .
CHRIS	yes?
THOMAS	if i don't forget all of it, you know. that would be kind of nice.
CHRIS	you do remember some.
THOMAS	because you're here. you know, right now.
CHRIS	and when i leave it will . . .
THOMAS	yes, it will all go too.
CHRIS	i know. i'm sorry.
THOMAS	it's not your fault.
CHRIS	still.
THOMAS	but you'll come back.
CHRIS	i don't know about that.
THOMAS	but we are good together.
CHRIS	we are not together. i have a husband.
THOMAS	but see, if you do, you can tell me exactly what happened last night. you know, how we met on the train and all that.
CHRIS	at the station.

THOMAS	see. that's exactly why i need you. and it will be fun. you can tell me what else we talked about.
CHRIS	i don't think that will happen.
THOMAS	it's okay. i know you will. maybe not soon. but
CHRIS	no.
THOMAS	Chris.
CHRIS	i'm sorry.
THOMAS	but you will leave me something.
CHRIS	like what?
THOMAS	i don't know. just something to remember you next time. until the next time.
CHRIS	i don't think i'll be coming back, Thomas. i can't lie to you.
THOMAS	you will.
CHRIS	no.
THOMAS	you don't have to go yet.
CHRIS	i do.
THOMAS	who's waiting for you?
CHRIS	i'm sorry. it's time for me to go now.
THOMAS	what will you leave me?
CHRIS	nothing.
THOMAS	Chris.
CHRIS	i can't
THOMAS	of course you can. something you won't miss. it's going to be here. in case you ever want it back. you can come and get it. stay another night.
CHRIS	no. i'm sorry.
THOMAS	–

CHRIS   not this time.

THOMAS   how else will you remember last night?

CHRIS   do you have to ask?

THOMAS   it would be

CHRIS   it would be easy to do it.
             i know.

THOMAS   it would.

CHRIS   like every other time.

THOMAS   –

CHRIS   but i can't. i have to say no. and it's not . . . but
               i can't.
             can you understand that?
             it's not that simple.
             people would find out. you know what it's like.
             sooner or later someone would notice. and they
               would find out.
             what would you do then? what would you tell
               them?

THOMAS   you'd come as a friend. nothing else.

CHRIS   no?
             what would you say?
             it's not how it seems? it's different with you?
             it just happened once. twice?
             it's different this time?
             or
             it wasn't what you intended to do?
             you didn't mean to? it's not how it sounds?
             do *you* hear how it sounds?
             –
             and they might believe you. who knows.
             people hear what they want to hear.
             they don't ask.
             they want to know if you're doing 'fine'. and
               you say you're fine.
             i'm fine.
             i'm fine.

| | you say it enough times |
| | and somehow that makes it all alright. |

THOMAS   Chris.

CHRIS   and even if they see it, you see, if somehow
          they see us, there's always an explanation. it
          can't be, it can't be how it looks. they catch
          a glimpse. overhear a conversation. even just
          a line – and it's too late, they've made up
          their minds. we can say nothing happened,
          but people see what they want to see, and it
          doesn't matter, doesn't matter what you say
          after that, or how many times you repeat it,
          you can keep repeating it until you bleed out.

THOMAS   –

CHRIS   just a happy couple.
          that's all they want to hear.
          it gives them hope. it says the whole thing is
              possible.
          somehow.
          that's what they need to believe. it makes it
              easier for them.
          doesn't matter what i say.

          you say i worry too much. and you say it like i
              shouldn't. you say there's nothing to worry
              about. and what we know is just between us.
              it's ours.
          like it's a good thing to have.
          no one else knows. just you and i.
          and sometimes we pretend that even we don't
              know.
          it makes it easier.
          maybe we can even forget all about it. forget it
              happened.
          you see, if only we know, and we forget, who
              can say it ever happened?
          after all, you say, it's just us. nothing big.
              nothing important, my dear.
          just us.

          but i can't.

and i don't know if you actually hear it.
if the words come out.
i say i can't, you say of course you can.
it doesn't take much effort. just stay, stay here
    with me.
it's not that hard.
don't have to move.
don't have to decide.
relax.
stay just one more night.
go to your bed.
we'll talk in the morning.
think about everything some other time.
things might be different this time.
you say
it's nice. it's warm. it's safe. it could be fun.
it doesn't matter if you're tired. if you're feeling
    numb.
it's me. stay.
staying doesn't demand any effort.
and you can always do the thinking some other
    time.
but i thought about it.
i had enough time.
it's too late now.

i can't. not this time.

She turns around. THOMAS *is not there any
more. Just an empty blanket around her.*

She is on her own.

Scene Three

Same.

It is the BOWMAN *family house.*

CHRIS *is on the sofa, curled up under a blanket.*

She sits up.

She folds the blanket, places it on the arm of the sofa exactly where it was at the beginning.

BOWMAN *enters.*

Stands there for a second looking at her.

She doesn't notice him. She is trying to make it look the way it was.

On the side table, there is a coffee cup.

She takes it, looking for a place to put it.

BOWMAN	i was looking for you.
CHRIS	–
BOWMAN	you weren't here.
CHRIS	i was.
BOWMAN	didn't you hear me?
CHRIS	no.
BOWMAN	i called.
CHRIS	did you?
BOWMAN	yes.
CHRIS	what did you want?
BOWMAN	where were you?
CHRIS	right here.

BOWMAN	here?
CHRIS	yes.
BOWMAN	alright.
CHRIS	–
BOWMAN	you got up early.
CHRIS	yes.
BOWMAN	and what were you doing?
CHRIS	nothing.
BOWMAN	you were doing nothing?
CHRIS	look, it's early. what do you want me to say. i wasn't doing anything important. i was just having my tea.

Pause.

BOWMAN	and how was it?
CHRIS	–
BOWMAN	well, was it nice?
CHRIS	it was.
BOWMAN	good. hot tea?
CHRIS	yes.
BOWMAN	not too hot, i hope?
CHRIS	–
BOWMAN	very good. so?
CHRIS	would you like me to make you some?
BOWMAN	no, thank you. i'm alright at the moment.
CHRIS	fine.
BOWMAN	and?

56

CHRIS	what?
BOWMAN	i take it everything is alright?
CHRIS	yes.
BOWMAN	you had a good night?
CHRIS	it was fine. thank you.
BOWMAN	good.
	Pause.
	so?
CHRIS	yes?
BOWMAN	aren't you going to ask me?
CHRIS	ask you what?
BOWMAN	how was my night?
CHRIS	–
BOWMAN	no?
CHRIS	i have to get ready.
BOWMAN	you don't have to.
CHRIS	i don't want to be late.
BOWMAN	i wouldn't worry about that.
CHRIS	we'll be late.
BOWMAN	we are not going.
CHRIS	sorry?
BOWMAN	we are not going anywhere today.
CHRIS	what do you mean?
BOWMAN	i called them. they know we won't be coming.
CHRIS	you didn't say anything.
BOWMAN	i'm telling you now.
CHRIS	they'll be waiting.
BOWMAN	they won't. i cancelled.

CHRIS	yes. i heard you the first time. but they will still be waiting for me. same as the last time.
BOWMAN	no.
CHRIS	you can't do that. it's too late now.
BOWMAN	i talked to them early this morning.
CHRIS	did you?
BOWMAN	i did.
CHRIS	and you just cancelled. you didn't ask me? didn't ask me at all?
BOWMAN	are you getting upset?
CHRIS	– i'm not. i would just like to know.
BOWMAN	i didn't feel like going today. so i'm not. – and you can't go without me, can you?
CHRIS	they are my parents.
BOWMAN	and they send you their love.
CHRIS	you
BOWMAN	yes?
CHRIS	what else did they say?
BOWMAN	they understand. your father is slightly worried about you, but he understands.
CHRIS	i'm sure he does.
BOWMAN	Christina.
CHRIS	yes?
BOWMAN	aren't you going to ask me?
CHRIS	what?
BOWMAN	how was my night?

CHRIS	don't do this.
BOWMAN	is it that hard?
CHRIS	–
BOWMAN	is it?
CHRIS	no.
BOWMAN	then you can do it.
CHRIS	don't.
BOWMAN	even you should be / able to
CHRIS	listen, i really / need to

He puts his hand – quickly but gently – to her face.

She freezes.

BOWMAN	didn't you hear me?

Pause.

CHRIS	i did.
BOWMAN	good.
CHRIS	i did. please.

He puts his hand down.

BOWMAN	you know i don't like doing this.
CHRIS	you say.
BOWMAN	trust me. i don't. and no, i didn't have a good night. would you like to know why?
CHRIS	–
BOWMAN	would you like to know why, my dear?
CHRIS	why?
BOWMAN	so you would? alright. – and you have no idea why?

CHRIS	no.
BOWMAN	you had a nice cup of tea then, didn't you?
CHRIS	i told you. it was alright.
BOWMAN	you must be very tired.
CHRIS	i'm fine.
BOWMAN	are you?
CHRIS	yes, i just told you. i'm fine.
BOWMAN	where did you sleep last night?
CHRIS	sorry?
BOWMAN	you didn't hear what i said?
CHRIS	i did.
BOWMAN	then answer me. not in the bedroom?
CHRIS	–
BOWMAN	no?
CHRIS	no.
BOWMAN	i noticed.
CHRIS	–
BOWMAN	and? what was the plan? are you going to tell me more?
CHRIS	tell you what?
BOWMAN	Christina.
CHRIS	tell you what?
BOWMAN	you spent the night here. on your sofa. didn't you?
CHRIS	what are you saying?
BOWMAN	you weren't in the bed.
CHRIS	i couldn't sleep.
BOWMAN	so you got up.

CHRIS	yes. i got up. is there something wrong with that?
BOWMAN	and had some tea.
CHRIS	coffee. coffee, actually.
BOWMAN	you don't drink coffee.
CHRIS	i felt like it.
BOWMAN	oh, did you?
CHRIS	–
BOWMAN	you made yourself a nice little cup of coffee then, didn't you?
CHRIS	yes, i did.
BOWMAN	and came to your sofa.
CHRIS	–
BOWMAN	yes?
CHRIS	yes.
BOWMAN	and then?
CHRIS	then what?
BOWMAN	what did you do then?
CHRIS	nothing. i just sat here for a bit. i was too tired to sleep.
BOWMAN	tired.
CHRIS	yes.
BOWMAN	you didn't go anywhere?
CHRIS	no.
BOWMAN	is that so?
CHRIS	what are you saying?
BOWMAN	and you slept well?
CHRIS	i didn't sleep much. i just told you. i couldn't sleep. that's why i was tired.
BOWMAN	but you are fine now.

CHRIS	yes. i'm fine.
BOWMAN	and then you decided to go to my bathroom.
CHRIS	what?
BOWMAN	my bathroom.
CHRIS	i didn't.
BOWMAN	no?
CHRIS	certainly not.
BOWMAN	are you saying you stayed – in your bed – all night?
CHRIS	on the sofa.
BOWMAN	your sofa.
CHRIS	yes.

He suddenly puts his hand on her cheek again. Just for a second. Then puts it down.

She immediately presses the cheek with her palm.

She doesn't move for a few moments.

Then removes her hand.

There's blood.

BOWMAN	you are lying, Christina.
CHRIS	you cut me.
BOWMAN	you lied.
CHRIS	you said you wouldn't do it any more.
BOWMAN	i've changed my mind.
CHRIS	you promised.
BOWMAN	and you promised not to touch anything that belongs to me, didn't you?
CHRIS	i didn't touch anything. i never went near.
BOWMAN	you took all my pills.

CHRIS	what?
BOWMAN	you emptied my bottle and put it right back where it was. didn't you?
CHRIS	no. of course not.
BOWMAN	why . . .
CHRIS	i didn't.
BOWMAN	. . . why do this when i can tell when you're lying?
CHRIS	i swear to you.
BOWMAN	you know i can.
CHRIS	–
BOWMAN	yes?
CHRIS	i didn't go anywhere near your bathroom.
BOWMAN	you put it back in its place and left me in bed. yes?
CHRIS	no. you were in bed. yes. i thought you were asleep. i came down to have a cup of but i never went . . . no.
BOWMAN	you came down here hoping i'd wake up. – on your lovely sofa.
CHRIS	no.
BOWMAN	hoping i would need them and there wouldn't be any.
CHRIS	no.
BOWMAN	there wasn't any.
CHRIS	it has nothing to do with me.
BOWMAN	i woke up. and you know what it's like.

CHRIS	there must be another bottle somewhere. in the bathroom. you just didn't see it. i could take a look. i could check right now.
BOWMAN	it's a very sharp pain, Christina. very sharp.
CHRIS	would you like me to go and check now?
BOWMAN	there's no need. my drawer is empty. same in the bathroom. none.
CHRIS	no.
BOWMAN	i called you. do you remember that?
CHRIS	i didn't hear you.
BOWMAN	were you hoping it would happen again?
CHRIS	i'm telling you i didn't hear you.
BOWMAN	did you . . .
CHRIS	no
BOWMAN	. . . did you think i was going to die this time?
CHRIS	no.
BOWMAN	did you really think i was that weak? that i was going to let you let me die?
CHRIS	you are talking . . . what are you talking about?
BOWMAN	i called you.
CHRIS	no
BOWMAN	Christina.
CHRIS	no.
BOWMAN	it was almost five before i could get up. and where were you?
CHRIS	no.
BOWMAN	you were here on your sofa, wrapped up in that blanket, hugging your mug, pretending –

CHRIS   i wasn't here.

BOWMAN   don't lie.
              you weren't in the bed.

CHRIS   i went out.

              Pause.

BOWMAN   excuse me?

CHRIS   i went out.

BOWMAN   you went out?

CHRIS   yes.

BOWMAN   out of the house?

CHRIS   yes. i wasn't here.

BOWMAN   is that what you're saying? that's the story now?

CHRIS   i'm telling you the truth. after we
              after you

              –

              i just couldn't stay here.
              i had to get out. you went back to the bedroom.
                and
              i took your keys and i went out.

BOWMAN   alright. alright.
              let's say you went out.

CHRIS   that's right. it was raining. but i went out.

BOWMAN   and where did you go?

CHRIS   –

BOWMAN   where did you go?

CHRIS   to see a friend.

BOWMAN   in the middle of the night?

CHRIS   it wasn't the middle of the night.

BOWMAN   what was it then?

CHRIS   –

BOWMAN	did you hear what i said?
CHRIS	stop talking to me like that.
BOWMAN	you don't listen otherwise.
CHRIS	it was late. yes. maybe. but it wasn't the middle of the night. i told you. i went to see a friend.
BOWMAN	oh don't be ridiculous. you don't have any friends.
CHRIS	stop it.
BOWMAN	well, do you?
CHRIS	–
BOWMAN	come on. tell me the truth. what did you do?
CHRIS	i told you. i went to see someone.
BOWMAN	alright.
CHRIS	a friend.
BOWMAN	a man?
CHRIS	–
BOWMAN	Christina.
CHRIS	so what if it was a man?
BOWMAN	i see. alright. fine.
CHRIS	what difference does it make?
BOWMAN	so? do i get to hear more? are you going to tell me? what was he like?
CHRIS	how do you mean, what was he like?
BOWMAN	was he good-looking? exciting? was he kind?
CHRIS	he was kind.

BOWMAN	i'm sure he was. and did he tell you how smart you are?
CHRIS	–
BOWMAN	how different you are?
CHRIS	–
BOWMAN	was he passionate?
CHRIS	it wasn't anything like that.
BOWMAN	but you still decided to spend the night.
CHRIS	i didn't stay.
BOWMAN	no?
CHRIS	i didn't spend the night with him.
BOWMAN	is that so?
CHRIS	i have to go now. i have to get ready. i'm going to see my parents tonight.
BOWMAN	will you pay attention for once? i told you. i cancelled.
CHRIS	i'm still going to see them.
BOWMAN	no, Christina. you are not.
CHRIS	stop calling me that.
BOWMAN	it's your name.
CHRIS	i don't want to talk any more.
BOWMAN	i'm very sorry, but i do.
CHRIS	you can't make me –

He touches her arm very lightly and leaves another tiny bloody cut.

BOWMAN	yes i can.
CHRIS	it hurts.
BOWMAN	it helps you concentrate.
CHRIS	it doesn't.

BOWMAN	you were telling me. about last night.
CHRIS	i told you already.
BOWMAN	tell me again.
CHRIS	–
BOWMAN	you say you didn't sleep here, and i'm just asking you where did you sleep then? i'm your husband. you live with me. you love me. i have the right to know. where did you spend the night?
CHRIS	with a friend.
BOWMAN	you just said you didn't.
CHRIS	with another friend.
BOWMAN	oh. another friend?
CHRIS	yes.
BOWMAN	alright. alright. so there is another one.
CHRIS	yes.
BOWMAN	and you spent the night with him?
CHRIS	yes.
BOWMAN	did you have sex with that one?
CHRIS	i didn't sleep with him. no. not like that.
BOWMAN	well, i'm surprised.
CHRIS	why are you doing this?
BOWMAN	so you didn't have sex with him?
CHRIS	no.
BOWMAN	and why not?
CHRIS	i'm married. you are my husband.

BOWMAN	i know i am. it's you who seems to forget.
CHRIS	how could i?
BOWMAN	tell me then.
CHRIS	–
BOWMAN	go on.
CHRIS	i couldn't sleep. alright. i needed to talk to someone. that's all. i didn't plan to stay. i went out just for a to clear my mind. i was coming back. but then it was late and it just i stayed, alright. there's nothing wrong in that. – i came back.
BOWMAN	to your sofa.
CHRIS	i came back home.
BOWMAN	why?
CHRIS	isn't that what you want? i'm here.
BOWMAN	after spending the night with two kind, gentle and understanding men. how nice.
CHRIS	i have the right.
BOWMAN	oh please.
CHRIS	don't.
BOWMAN	you have no idea what happened, do you?
CHRIS	i know exactly what happened. i just told you.
BOWMAN	why do you always make me do this?
CHRIS	don't.
BOWMAN	i have to.

CHRIS   you don't.

BOWMAN   i do. or you just wander off. you need to
            concentrate, Chris.
            come on, it's not that hard.

CHRIS   –

BOWMAN   tell me.

CHRIS   there's nothing to tell.

BOWMAN   what really happened last night?

CHRIS   you can't understand that other people can be
            nice to me, can you?
            that they are.
            is that what's bothering you?
            or is it
            how hard is it to understand that someone can
            be nice to me?

BOWMAN   and you don't know the reason? you have no
            idea why?

CHRIS   because they are kind. as people. that's all.
            they don't have to be, but they are.
            that's why. not like us.

BOWMAN   oh come on. no one's that stupid. not even you.

CHRIS   i can talk to them.
            they like me.

BOWMAN   no they don't.

CHRIS   and how would you know? you weren't there.

BOWMAN   you just make them that way. make them in
            your head. make them like you for a while.

CHRIS   they are not like you.

BOWMAN   i know. i'm real. unfortunately.

CHRIS   no.

BOWMAN   don't be angry with me.
            it's not my fault if they are gone now.

CHRIS   i left. not them.
               it was my decision.

BOWMAN   was it?

CHRIS   yes.

BOWMAN   ah. and now you are proud?

CHRIS   –

BOWMAN   look, it's time to stop this.
               –
               you know that, don't you?

CHRIS   you can't tell me what to do.

BOWMAN   i can. i am your husband.

CHRIS   you hurt me.

BOWMAN   you hurt me too.

CHRIS   how?

BOWMAN   you tried last night.

CHRIS   i didn't.
               i wasn't here.
               i was with someone else.

BOWMAN   i know what you did.
               and i don't have to prove it. not to you.

CHRIS   you're losing your mind.

BOWMAN   don't say that. sounds odd coming from you.

CHRIS   i need to get ready.

BOWMAN   for Christ sake. don't you ever listen to what
                   i say?

CHRIS   i know you called them.
               don't worry.
               i'm not going to go there.
               they won't find out.

BOWMAN   so what are you getting ready for?

CHRIS   i'm leaving.

BOWMAN	yes. you said so. many times. you're going to get ready. and then you're going to leave. i heard you. and where are you going to go?
CHRIS	i'll find someplace.
BOWMAN	don't be ridiculous.
CHRIS	i'm not.
BOWMAN	you have nowhere to go.
CHRIS	i'll be alright.
BOWMAN	you know you won't leave.
CHRIS	i will.
BOWMAN	you never do.
CHRIS	–
BOWMAN	what? do we have to go through this every single time? you do something stupid. i ask you why. you threaten to leave. i explain why you can't. and then you cry.
CHRIS	–
BOWMAN	i'll make your bed for you.
CHRIS	you don't have to.
BOWMAN	you need to rest.
CHRIS	i'm fine.
BOWMAN	you can keep repeating that *He steps towards her.* for as long as you want.
CHRIS	don't.
BOWMAN	i'm not going to hurt you.
CHRIS	you're going to cut me.

BOWMAN   i promise.
                come here.
                –
                come here.

CHRIS   –

BOWMAN   look. i'm not upset. i know it's hard.
                but it will be alright.
                yes?
                i'll make the bed. you can get some sleep.
                you'll wake up in a few hours and everything
                    will be alright.

CHRIS   it won't.

BOWMAN   i promise.

CHRIS   –

BOWMAN   you're tired.
                you had a bad day.
                and a hard night.

CHRIS   –

BOWMAN   didn't you?

CHRIS   i did.

BOWMAN   i know what it's like.
                it hasn't been easy for you. all this.
                it's exhausting. it makes you feel tired.

CHRIS   –

BOWMAN   doesn't it?

CHRIS   it does.

BOWMAN   why don't you just rest.
                you need that, don't you?

CHRIS   i do.

BOWMAN   and we can talk when you wake up.

                He goes to her.

                come here.

73

CHRIS	–
BOWMAN	it's me, Chris.
CHRIS	–
BOWMAN	hey. it's alright. it will be alright. – i know it can be hard. but you know. it's us. we'll get through it. right?
CHRIS	–
BOWMAN	you know we will. we always do. it will be fine.
CHRIS	why can't you just be kind?
BOWMAN	Chris.
CHRIS	can you show me your hands?
BOWMAN	look
CHRIS	please. show me your hands.
BOWMAN	there's nothing. see. nothing there.
CHRIS	why do you do it?
BOWMAN	–
CHRIS	why do you hurt me?
BOWMAN	you know i love you.
CHRIS	–
BOWMAN	i do.
CHRIS	–
BOWMAN	i woke up. and you weren't there. and i just got i was thinking where are you. i started thinking where you could be.

and it was too much.

–

i was afraid. i didn't know how to ask.

–

i didn't mean to hurt you.

He touches her. She flinches but lets him.

She's not harmed.

you understand that, don't you?
you know how it feels.

CHRIS   i do.

BOWMAN   see. we understand each other.
and you understand that i have to
sometimes i have to help you – concentrate.

CHRIS   no.

BOWMAN   it helps you –

CHRIS   it doesn't help me concentrate. stop it. i'm fine.

BOWMAN   don't talk to me like that.

CHRIS   it's too late.
people know now.

BOWMAN   what people?

CHRIS   they see what's happening here.

BOWMAN   they can't.

CHRIS   don't be naive.
you thought no one will ever find out.

BOWMAN   who is they?

CHRIS   they can see me with my shirt off, cleaning my
          cuts.
through the window.
from outside.
you can't keep it secret for ever.
they see cuts on me.
when they touch me they notice blood.

BOWMAN   there is no them.

CHRIS	you think i'm worthless without you?
BOWMAN	can you prove to me that you are not?
CHRIS	–
BOWMAN	–
CHRIS	can you tell me why i should stay?
BOWMAN	– you wouldn't be happy without me.
CHRIS	i was happy last night.
BOWMAN	it was a dream.
CHRIS	you weren't there.
BOWMAN	i need you. i needed you last night.
CHRIS	you say.
BOWMAN	come here.
CHRIS	stay away from me.
BOWMAN	you don't mean that.
CHRIS	stay away
BOWMAN	Christina.
CHRIS	go away.
BOWMAN	Christina
CHRIS	go away!

There is a loud bang on the door behind her.

She steps away from the door.

BOWMAN   (*offstage, on the other side of the door*)
Christina.

She looks at BOWMAN *on stage, not sure if he is there.*

He is still standing there, quiet, unmoving. Not saying anything.

BOWMAN   (*offstage*) Christina. can you hear me?

CHRIS	–
BOWMAN	(*offstage*) Christina.
CHRIS	i can't.
BOWMAN	(*offstage*) Chris. open the door.
CHRIS	i can't. not this time.
BOWMAN	(*offstage*) Chris.
CHRIS	and you know why. – it would be easy to do it. i know. like every other time.
BOWMAN	–

CHRIS	but i can't. i have to say no. and it's not . . . but
	    i can't.
	can you understand that?
	it's not that simple.
	people would find out. you know what it's like.
	sooner or later someone would notice. and they
	    would find out.
	what would you do then? what would you tell
	    them?

BOWMAN	(*offstage*) Chris. you can't do this.
CHRIS	no? what would you say? it's not how it seems? it's different with you? it just happened once. twice? it's different this time? or it wasn't what you intended to do? you didn't mean to? it's not how it sounds? do *you* hear how it sounds? – and they might believe you. who knows. people hear what they want to hear. they don't ask.

they want to know if you're doing 'fine'. and
    you say you're fine.
i'm fine.
i'm fine.
you say it enough times
and somehow that makes it all alright.

BOWMAN   (*offstage*) Chris.

CHRIS   and even if they see it, you see, if somehow
    they see us, there's always an explanation.
    it can't be, it can't be how it looks. they catch
    a glimpse. overhear a conversation. even just
    a line – and it's too late, they've made up
    their minds. we can say nothing happened,
    but people see what they want to see, and it
    doesn't matter, doesn't matter what you say
    after that, or how many times you repeat it,
    you can keep repeating it until you bleed out.

BOWMAN   –

CHRIS   just a happy couple.
    that's all they want to hear.
    it gives them hope. it says the whole thing is
    possible.
    somehow.
    that's what they need to believe. it makes it
    easier for them.
    doesn't matter what i say.

BOWMAN   (*offstage*) Chris.

CHRIS   you say i worry too much. and you say it like
    i shouldn't. you say there's nothing to worry
    about. and what we know is just between us.
    it's ours.
    like it's a good thing to have.
    no one else knows. just you and i.
    and sometimes we pretend that even we don't
    know.
    it makes it easier.
    maybe we can even forget all about it. forget it
    happened.

you see, if only we know, and we forget, who
    can say it ever happened?

after all, you say, it's just us. nothing big.
    nothing important, my dear.

just us.

BOWMAN   –

CHRIS   but i can't.

and i don't know if you actually hear it.

if the words come out.

i say i can't, you say of course you can.

it doesn't take much effort. just stay, stay here
    with me.

it's not that hard.

don't have to move.

don't have to decide.

relax.

stay just one more night.

go to your bed.

we'll talk in the morning.

think about everything some other time.

things might be different this time.

you say

it's nice. it's warm. it's safe. it could be fun.

it doesn't matter if you're tired. if you're feeling
    numb.

it's me. stay.

staying doesn't demand any effort.

and you can always do the thinking some other
    time.

but i thought about it.

i had enough time.

it's too late now.

i can't.

not this time.

i'm done.

There is no more noise coming from outside.

Long pause.

She goes to the sofa.

She sits down.

She is finished.

A moment.

My name is Mrs Bowman.

Pause.

I'm here to see my husband.

End.

Scottish Anthologies from Nick Hern Books

SCOT-FREE
New Scottish Plays
edited by Alasdair Cameron

Writer's Cramp
John Byrne

Losing Venice
John Clifford

The Letter Box
Ann Marie di Mambro

Elizabeth Gordon Quinn
Chris Hannan

Dead Dad Dog
John McKay

Saturday at the Commodore
Rona Munro

The Steamie
Tony Roper

SCOTLAND PLAYS
New Scottish Drama
edited by Philip Howard

Wormwood
Catherine Czerkawska

Brothers of Thunder
Ann Marie di Mambro

Passing Places
Stephen Greenhorn

One Way Street
David Greig

Quelques Fleurs
Liz Lochhead

One Good Beating
Linda McLean

Lazybed
Iain Crichton Smith

A Nick Hern Book

Night Time first published in Great Britain as a paperback original in 2007 by Nick Hern Books Limited, 14 Larden Road, London W3 7ST in association with the Traverse Theatre, Edinburgh

Night Time copyright © 2007 Selma Dimitrijević

Selma Dimitrijević has asserted her right to be identified as the author of this work

Cover design: Ned Hoste, 2H

Typeset by Country Setting, Kingsdown, Kent CT14 8ES
Printed in Great Britain by CPI Bookmarque, Croydon CR0 4TD

A CIP catalogue record for this book is available from the British Library

ISBN   978 1 85459 586 7